A LIFE OF SMALL CRIME

David Lawrence

Cyberwit.net
HIG 45 Kaushambi Kunj, Kalindipuram
Allahabad - 211011 (U.P.) India
http://www.cyberwit.net
Tel: +(91) 9415091004
E-mail: info@cyberwit.net

Contents

The Sweat of Summer

I am disappearing into the sweat of summer as I clog all my
pipes with tired water.

I am yesterday's failure and tomorrow's
Indifference.

I don't care that I am disappearing into the air;
I am death's puppet;
I am torn *papier Mache.*

I don't know how I stand up when my spirits are beneath the
ground in a cave where batman is dead.

It is a hundred degrees in the boxing gym and I am melting
Like butter in a sandwich left in the back seat of a car.

Teaching and Writing Poems at Gleason's Gym

I have a five-hour break in teaching at the gym and I am broken
by my diminished number of students and my lack of popularity
when I should be delightful.

So I go into my office to write my millionth poem and
To get in touch with being out of touch
In a smudge on a glass.

I have so much nothing to say that it keeps coming out of my
mouth like secrets
Shared among the silence of intention.

If I get really in touch with myself I tickle
My ribs and laugh like surrender
Like appreciation
Like love.

It's good to be me and not you whoever you are and the compat-
ibility is a gesture
Of respect to the God that invented me for His amusement.

Gladiators

The difference is not bright but dull sprinkles on the cake of encumbrance surrounded by cream. I know who you are by the long distance that shuffles between us. Sorry that I can't fathom the fish or the deep sea diver. I am a clam on the bottom of the sea. I put Tabasco on myself and eat the meat. The taste of my death is good. I do not beat the meat. I'm getting a little old for that. I am the surprise that becomes routine and I can never face myself in the mirror when the glass is broken. I have fought gladiators in the hopes of getting into the movies but have died at the trials and never sold tickets. Did you know that I was knocked out cold in my first pro fight in Denver? I didn't feel it. I was asleep. When I woke up a doctor was shining a flashlight in my eyes. Thank me for not being you so that you can relish yourself while I cry into a linen tablecloth.

My Road

I am coming to the end of my road and I wonder whether I will
fall off a cliff or be forced to climb five miles straight up into a
blizzard.

I know what I know which is nothing
Of relevance and little
Of import.

This life was something else and I could never keep my hands on
its coattails;
I am dropped from a cliff like a bug.

What was I doing here when I was doing nothing I could define?
Purpose eludes me and I am lost in a papoose
Like a child of God.

Life is what you have stolen from me and I am the empty
pockets of failure. I don't care whether I climb the stairs or the
banister falls on my head
And knocks me out.

I have lived as a surprise and never
Known the purpose of my neglect
Or my intention.

It's been a rare trip and I am glad that the tracks permitted me to
ride their direction to an indefinite conclusion.

Bipolar in the Diner

It's nice to feel your life is meaningless and to roll it up into a
sock and put your foot on your head.

Who cares?
I put distance between my concern and my interpretation
Of feeling.

It is embarrassing to love oneself but it is better than committing
suicide from the bridge of other people's disdain.

I am all wrapped up in myself like a bipolar breakdown.
I am a rocket to the moon.
I am everything that you could be if you could be me.

I am an omelet of manic eggs beneath a dash of salt of blind
depression in an empty diner without customers.

Politics

Politics is an angry field where there are no flowers; just thorns and bees ripping into your chinos. Every gardenia denies a rose and only admits to its own pealed intelligence. Flowers battle in the garden and give their stupid opinions of oppositional petals. I'd like to take the hose and drown the political positions of pansies. I don't give a darn about your praise of the wrong president. I'd rather vote for myself than some glamorous jerk that puts his face on a flag. It's strange that politicians have no talent. They can't paint, draw, sing, act, do scientific experiments or do anything either than read speeches to a stubborn audience. Imagine using a megaphone to influence dummies. Charlie McCarthy doesn't have his own voice. He is a throwaway. We are at a party for dunces. It's idiots that feel so strongly about themselves that they grab their beliefs by the throat and strangle them. I'd rather die out of office than be a goon who officiates the state.

Moping Trainer

If I had something to do I would do it but it eludes me and I find
myself playing with my fingers.

I yarn my thumbs like wool
And knit a sweater
Out of boredom.

Seventy-one years old and I am hanging around a gym hoping for
more students.
Am I ignored because of the sags in my face or because of my
small bald spot?

I can still do fifty chins and curl eighty pounds on a barbell.
I fought on national television and
Was ranked as a welterweight.

And the other trainers who never fought in Vegas flock their
students around them like sheep.

On the intelligence side,
I was a college professor and a Ph.D.
Fifteen published books.

The lessons you could learn from me are intellectual athleticism.
I once was the best salesman in the insurance industry and now I
can't sell myself.

I am too good to be good. I don't have much of a following.

Not Proud

I hang out at Gleason's Gym waiting for students to show up. They come and go but mostly go. Gone is a reference to the past, present and the disappearance of tomorrow. I am gone before they arrive because I am water spilled from a bottle. I am the disappearance of disappearance into the presence of absence like hair through a comb. You know me for whom I am not and I am not, a lot, and a little of effervescence. Death be not proud. What the hell does that mean? Everyone else wants to be proud—gays, transgenders and amputees. I prefer depression to pride. The loveliness of self-deprecation. Why can't death rise up to the occasion like all the underprivileged? I am proud. I don't care if you think I should be ashamed. I am the rise of the fall in the bloat of pride. I am tomorrow's glance in the mirror of good looks. At 71 that's hard to say. Unless it's the boast of another lie. Unless I am the predilection of a future face lift. Never. I celebrate my drabness. I am the intellectual space between my wrinkles. I am proud that I am not proud.

Shakespeare and Me

I gargle my thoughts so that I swallow down the mucous of my
intelligence.
I am worried about leaving this earth
And arriving on the green cheese of the moon
In a saucer cup.
I am outer space in a wispy glow among craters and deceased
thoughts.
When I die will I cry?
Not after.
But before I might in anticipation.
I am waiting for our nation to fall into civil war and death
Become a hiatus in life.
The spaces I inhabit arc libraries of indigo knowledge.
I rip the spines of the books so that I am bewildered by smudged
pages.
I hope that mercy falls gentle as the rain because Shakespeare
Is the last and only poet.
Except me.
I am not as explicable but I am more profound than iambic
pentameter.

Can't Be Touched

Sometimes I can't follow my thoughts up the stairs as I trip on
the rug runner and fall on my nose.

I am everything magnificent and as wonderful
As a moose head on the wall.

I know myself like
A neighbor
I lived next to for twenty years
In the suburbs.

I really don't want to meet you because I am in no need of
distractions and live within my own dominion like a king.

Stay away from me so that I can be
Me without the intrusion
Of your remarks
And the friendliness of your disrespect.

I will dance with myself on the parapets of the castle and put on
a knight's armor so that I can't be touched.

California Carmen

If you knew Carmen like I knew Carmen you'd want to be her neighbor.
But her neighbor is looking for fights.
So when Carmen's dog takes a leak on the neighbor's plants
She bitches, "I just planted those at great expense."
What expense?
It's a plant.
How about the expense of the insult to Carmen?
And yet Carmen is demure and polite,
She says, "I'm sorry. I understand…"
What's to understand?
The rudeness of the plant lady?
The neighbor says "Do you even speak English"
What difference does her language make?
Why doesn't she ask her if she can sip the moon through a straw?
So much irrelevance in the plant lady's lament.
I taught Carmen to fight at Gleason's Gym.
But she takes the high road and says to her neighbor,
"Excuse me but do you realize what you just said is deeply offensive to me"
The woman is mortified but I wish she would be mortally dead.
Rudeness should not be allowed to fester near the garden.
Carmen is better than the insults thrown at her.

Through a Flavor Straw

I am wrong but I don't know it because I like to think that I am a
right turn on an exit ramp.

I get off where I go and I enter
The fabulous punctuation
Of maybe.

Tomorrow is not yet mine but it will become my possession like a
fresh new pair of shoes.

What's the difference whether I am right
Or wrong as long as I am breathing
Through a flavor straw
And tasting the chocolate of the stars.

I'm coming towards the end of the end and I wrap myself up in
celluloid like a classic film.

I don't know myself because I am someone different and
I look forward towards my camouflage and
Not being recognized.

A Sad Mood

A sad mood predicts my tears and dictates the future of moods
and the attitudes that I can't spare.

So if I cry without cause don't be shocked
That you are getting wet
In my weather.

You'd be better to ignore me because I don't want you getting
caught in a downpour of my twisted love.

Sometimes I am so sad for no reason that I sneeze on a linen
handkerchief and get the stitching in my eye.

It has nothing to do with what comes
And goes and the fatness
Of the weather.

It is my chemistry that juggles the balls of opposition and finds an
audience for its clowning behavior.

A Real Feel

It's not that love is so magnificent but it is that I love magnificence and the feeling I feel is the real feel.

You startle me when you drop your eyes
On me like jelly beans.
You are strong like Ronald Regan.

Loving myself like a manic occasion I am as resilient as a helium balloon flying over the Alps.

When we are together I am elevated into a new level of incompetent wonder and catch myself by the scruff of strength.

It's all about love and the simple things
I find in the complexity of a woman.

When I entered grammar school I knew that I wanted to marry a girl and that to go against the grain was to let the rain fall down on me like buckshot.

I had my first crush at seven and we even kissed a little. Her name might have been Linda and we lived on Linda Drive.

I feel weak. I am weak. I am knocking on the mouse hole of death hoping to get out the other side.

SONG

If the song comes back to the throat it will get swallowed in
intention and the beat will be broken.

I don't want to hear music.
I don't want you to sing at me like
A slingshot.

I want the silence of a raisin in its brown creases raised on oil
and the penumbra of taste.

Take your band and throw it
In the river.
Let your music drown.

Don't waste your song on me because I am not interested in the
music of nonsense when I am trying to listen in to my own
thoughts.

Going Nowhere

I never want to travel again because I have entered the retreat
of myself and found love wrapped in my own arms.

I don't give a damn about a Chinaman
Or a Parisian crepe.
I am me and only me and I am American
Dancing without Paris.

I don't want to leave my house nor to open the doors into a world
that is foreign and fast in its retreat from my introspection.

Keep your voice down because I don't
Want to hear your stupidity
And your lack of ideas.

I am so in love with myself that I understand the perspective of
looking into my heart and hearing the beating of the blood.

Space Words

I have known less than the dictionary in space with its little
words and definitions.

I am not the meat and potatoes
Between the covers
Of Webster's.

Is that the Oxford English Dictionary or the typescript of outer
space
Defining itself?

I read the stars.
I play the grammar of Mars.
I am tomorrow
In the punctuation of today.

It's not the meaning that reminds me that I am myself but the
linguistic bundle of babble in its own tower.

Seventy-one

So I am seventy-one and am lucky to have another decade or two to go.

One two buckle my shoe
Before I am caught
In death's laces.

Not much more time to go before I go into that disappearance which is a kind of protection.

It's not that I want to die
But that I want to get
Out of here like
Thumbs putting out candle flames.

I was brought onto this earth to be part of its literature and if I failed I am assailed by sadness in a conch shell.

The Beauty of Hate

The beauty of hate is that it is so concrete and definite. It is focused and solid as a brick in my summer house wall. It is not airy fairy and indefinable like love. What is love? It's a vague impounding feeling. It's softness or aggression. It's wanting to devour another person so that she becomes part of you. It's changeable and you can't tell the anger and the passion from the gentleness. There is nothing beautiful about vagueness. I want to be firm. I want to hate which is a piece of love with directorial imperative. Love has no love to it. It is a lukewarm form of hate. Let me hate you. Let me love the rabid taste of disdain. Love is merely water in a strainer. It pours out into indefiniteness. It might not even be real. It doesn't have the veritas of hate.

My Family

I have lived as a moon and lit up your life like a sun. I am my father's son. I am bored by fun.

I come back to you like
An arrival from yesterday in a sling
Shot.

I am all the planets and a galaxy of thoughts that precede me in outer space.

I don't know if there is water
On the moon but I am a puddle
Near my space ship.

I am part of a family in which the parents are dead and my brother is still kicking like the Rockets.

And then there is my newer family,
My wife and son. I am dumped
Into the future.

I can't live without being surrounded by others. Not a communist village but a human family makes a nuclear explosion of love.

Who I Am

I know things that I don't know because confusion is my dear
delight and I am askew on a table of ankles.

What after all is all about
When about turns face
And leaves me
In confusion,
Profusion of madness.

I sometimes don't know who I am and I see myself as a figure
outside of me walking shoeless in the park.

I am breaking down into a failure
Of consciousness
The way the wind blows
In a canyon,
In a canon,
In death.

Death is poaching butterflies in a sticky hand and the modicum of
insanity when they are put in a glass Jar where life Is a failure to
open the cap.

In A Lung Deflation

The wrong with the right is a definition of surprise short of breath
in a lung deflation.

I met you in second grade.
Not really.
It was another girl who you would later
Look like.

All my life I have tried to get along with your getting along and
stopped you in your tracks like a rabbit in the garden.

So much divorce out there
And I am married
Forty-seven years like an endless
Tape measure.

There is something comfortable about your being my couch and
our being pillowed down with emotion where we watch television
without sound.

Someone Else's Joke

So I go ha-ha-ha and laugh at myself as if I were someone else's joke rather than the last laugh on myself.

I know you because you are me
And familiarity is a disease
That cures itself
In death.

Life is a bubble I dance upon as I rise into space blown from a pipe on the wind in the rain.

Identity is something that slips from me in a bandstand and the music is apparent and wonderful beneath the dampening of the carpet.

Nice to know me when I don't.
And good to see my face when I am blind.
I put my face in a feed bag
Like a horse pulling a knife sharpening carriage
In the nineteen forties.

Nice to be me when I am still trying to catch up with myself and take meaning out of porridge in a spoon.

On the Merry-Go-Round

There is meaning that is not meaning that is an oboe playing itself
in a parking lot.
I am a jerk.
Not really.

I don't know whether I am dreaming or awake or the space
between two comas in a description of a drafty corridor in a
burned-out building.

And so I look at myself and see nothing but intention overriding
dissipation.

I am coming to the end of the diving board
And am trying to get my courage up to dive into the concrete.

Krauthammer broke his neck and led a productive life.
He was a pundit wunderkind.

I have done less with a strong spine and every advantage in a
scoop of brilliance.

Death is approaching me on a merry-go-round and it seems like
fun when
The Fun House isn't burning down.

Time

There are times and there are other than the tick of the tock.
I am free.

I gather daisies of death in a basket
Like Little Bo Beep.

Seventy-one years old and so little to go that I am startled
By my brevity.

I come and go like tomorrow
And find meaning in the disappearance of language
And the trash of knowledge.

You come back to me like a guest at a funeral.
You just want to take one last look.

The flower on my button will take on a bce and I will be stung
By death near the hors d'oevres.

Clams on a Necklace

Where I am going is where you have gone. We repeat ourselves like radishes. I am in love with your cold cheek and feel like I will become part of the ice. Yes, we do what we do but we can't find distance in a near colloquy. I wonder where I will be in a few years. Is death a necessity or an accident? What difference does it make if you drown in shallow water. I put clams on a necklace and wear them around my neck. The tunnel leads to the grape and I find the wolf there. If I went up in that flying saucer I would be able to put the tea cup in it. My youth is over there in that trashcan like when I used to roll down the hill at Camp Birchwood in the garbage. The who thing matters down to you. You are the meaning of my paragraph and the choice of my sentences. It's been fun. It's great. It's me at summer camp in 1962.

A Broken Tree

Can't keep myself down even though I want to be subterranean.
I just keep bubbling to the surface
Like a child's pipe.

You know me for who I am but not who I am not.
Fun is fun but it can also be a distraction from meaning and
wanting.

I see you as you are and wonder why I am looking.
Trouble is a broken tree on a pathway.

I have leaves on my beard.
I am the beard of the elf in the forest.

I am the old man who wakes up wondering why he is alive.

Fish Tank

When I saw my shrink today I expanded like a child's balloon
and went up into the air like a helium attack.

I was panic in a panic and didn't know where I was
Or wasn't
In a split collage of personality.

You know me for whom I am not and I know me for whatever
definition I can pick from the fish tank.

A ball of my brain bounced against
My skull and I was less than
I figured
And more than I could imagine.

I don't know what I drew out of my shrink's office but it calmed
me like a skinned bass and the sound of a bass oboe.

Flavor

There is juice in the space container and it is the energetic
orange of bursting flavor.

I am getting bored with life
And want to sleep awhile
Like Rumpelstiltskin.

If I could hook up with a sleeping beauty I would find a life in a
seashell and know what the meaning of the beach engendered.

I yawn to find degradation in death
And hope it comes sooner
Than later.

Nice of you to imitate me so that I will find a second life in your
mirroring me and a morning in the sun lifting up its shades.

It's not the meaning that douses the eradication but the fun that
frolics on the beach on a boring summer vacation.

The Tail on the Horse

You are interested in the disappearance of meaning because absence makes the heart grow fonder. You have put your ear on my chest and found that love is beating. It is the physicality of emotional drizzle. You are you who is not me but I find your grandiosity is your distance from my occlusion. You are the majesty of a sunrise on a microscope. I am not ignoring you. That implies intention. I am entering your face like your own eyelash. I am proximate mascara. I am your eyeliner. The closer we get to each other the more we find distance in proximity and the tail on the horse swirls around. We don't need a stable when we have a trough. You are at a distance where you come closer to me. You are me. I don't know if there is any difference.

Time is a Lotion

I have fun in the sun and sun surrounds my fun like a diesel
engine at the cost of cheap gas.

You are the reason that I am without reason
And the knucklehead I wear
Is a dare
At madness.

Come on over to my house and you will discover that it is your
house and you will own me like a vote for the presidency.

Time is a lotion that I spread on my face
To anticipate the wrinkles
Of illegitimacy.

The other day I found twenty four hours in my pocket and knew
that I'd be carrying the weight of the day in my linen.

Pick Daisies

I pick daisies from your hair and find that blond is a friendly color
when I am lonely for your company.

I visit you through the back door
Because I don't want to give you an excuse
To lock it.

I lock myself up in your arms because I want to be protected
from my loneliness in the heart of your heart,
Your beating….

Pick me out of the bunch as I pick daisies from your hair and in
the pickings there is good and the gathering of lips.

It's not that I can't keep away from you
But that well, I don't really know
The meaning of distance.

Love is the elbow knocking of confusion when I don't know the
meaning of attraction in the old prairie among coyotes.

Marc

I haven't seen my old friend from high school since May flowers in the boxes along the avenues in New York City. He goes to Sag Harbor for the summer. It's now September and life breathes itself into the balloon of activity in our city. Marc never lost his business. He didn't go to jail like I did. He wasn't a man. He didn't pound his chest in celebration of his own toughness. I am Tarzan or the ape. I am proud of my lousy two jail years. Although I wish I hadn't been a short termer. I wish I had been executed. I am Meursault hoping death would curse me out. I hate myself. I want to be punished. Death be pliant and lead me into the next coffin. I want to be a *Stranger* to myself. I want to not recognize me. I want to escape the conscience of my face and not know what it means to have an identity. I am not a member of the white race. I am a Horse of no colors in the wizardry of Oz. I am not a Jew. I am not a not. I am an am. My heritage escapes me like a runaway horse on a bridle path. Marc goes back with me fifty-five years. We are starting and finishing together. The end is nigh. Ay, ay, captain of the finish, tail of the ending. I am a turd at the Bethpage stables. I am the saddle of the infinite.

Snuggle

I am sent to the event of my own quintessence and dear to me I
am in the wind, the rain and the hurricane.

I snuggle up with myself
Like a lobster pinching himself
With his own claw.

I have seen what I have seen and been what I have been but
never seen what I have been because I am elusive.

I have known me for seventy-one years
And been closer to myself
Than my elbow is to my sleeve.

Let the poem knows what it does and be a kite over my person-
ality as I fly to the thunder of personal ear drums.

Long Simmering

Sometimes you can't figure me out and in that we are the same
in lack of understanding.

I figure you out.
You are that person who fails
To understand me.

I am apparent, transparent. Can't you see that I am the pup that
follows after you hoping to get a taste of your biscuit.

When you spend fifty years together
You don't have much change
Or retrograde left.

I can understand why I am in love with you but can't figure what
you see in me. Do you have special binoculars to bring to the
distance a sort of cosmic thinking.

Dad

I don't know how long my dad is dead. I don't believe in details.
What difference does time make when he is a forever corpse in
the future?

He was my favorite person.
I wanted to be him even though he was only five
Foot five.

He was my miniature hero and I imagine him in the glass menag-
erie of my dreams as an undercurrent of drama.

I have a tape recording of his last message
To be on the phone
Where he tells me he loved me.
Beautiful is as beautiful says.

But I never rerecord the message or write it down because I
want to let him go into outer space without being stuck in sticki-
ness of my gooey love.

In A Glass Jar

I know things that I don't know because confusion is my dear
delight and I am askew on a table of ankles.

What after all is it all about
When about turns face
And leaves me
In confusion,
A profusion of madness.

I sometimes don't know who I am and I see myself as a figure
outside of me walking shoeless in the park.

I am breaking down into a failure
Of consciousness
The way the wind blows
In a canyon,
In a canon,
In death.

So this is what death is like— a failure to catch butterflies in a
sticky hand and the modicum of sanity in a glass jar.

Married

Things that drag dreary are like rain falling from a darkening sky which means meaning is not robust and sadness flies like a dead seagull. I have found you in the caboose, only there was no train except the train on your wedding dress. I was part of that. I was the stooge in the tuxedo who was amazed at what I was doing and where I was going and the first steps towards death. There is something about my funny bone that is not funny. Bone is death is death is bone. I am afraid of tomorrow's blood yet I welcome it. I want to embrace the nonchalance of absence at the core of disappearance. What I leave behind is myself and myself has often been an antagonist and difficult persuasion to false optimism. Let me review my life. It's been pretty good. There have been better. There have been worse. I will find a piece of peace in a jawbone of death. I am David. I am what you have been afraid to be. As I rattle on I almost forget you. But we are married until death brings us together.

Diversity

You are as stupid as your opinions and wise it would be to negate
your attitudes before they gel.

I've had enough of you
And your prejudices
Which are less than their solidity
And more than their bigotry.

What I hate about diversity is diversity and praising it is fear of
the milk carton of homogeneity. If you can't be who you be you
be distance from who you are.

The world would be better if it were one race—
either black, yellow, white or red.
The solidity of opinion
Is the death of ridiculous dispersion?

Or perhaps we should erase varieties so that we can love the
homogenous nature of being being in all its thickness.

Fifty Years

Love is not quite contrary because it is inflatable in its fashion
and breathable as a balloon.

It's what we are when we aren't
And what we can be
When we are not.

I have known you for fifty years and I am just starting to get sad
about pulling away from you.

I want to come close to your distance
And arrive at your happenstance,
A raindrop in a puddle.

I know you for what you are not and what you are not is your
approximation to my violent amelioration.

Here I am.
Here you are.
We are all here on a carousel of stampeding horses.

Back in East Meadow

A lot passes you by when you are sitting on a suburban curb licking an ice cream cone. The ice cream drips onto your sneaker laces and you realize that you have cold feet and don't want to engage. You are young, living in your parents' house with a brother and a dog. My dog was a beagle. We called her Cracker. I miss her sad eyes. I miss her floppy ears. I miss her wanting to hang out with me like a high school reunion. I miss the sun in June. I miss the bees that didn't always bite me. I miss the intensity of missing what I was missing. I miss being able to distinguish you from me. I miss assuming who I was without failing to approach myself in a field. I miss knowing what it was to have a heavy heart instead of the frivolity of indifference. Youth was the delight of unconsciousness and the failure to take myself seriously. I count the days or the months or the years until my death and don't give much of a damn if the damn breaks and floods me into drowned unconsciousness. I suppose it was fun to be me and whatever I wasn't I was. I am walking on water. I am not Christ. I am unreligious pontoons. I am a good athlete. Perhaps I am water skiing. Perhaps I am perhaps in a wonderland of maybe. I miss my adolescence. I miss the sun shining on my ice cream in The Meadow.

Life

This life is beginning to feel like the end of life and I am racing
towards nowhere-ville in a 57 Chevy.

I remember the rumbling of rumbles
In the parking lot
At Weston's.

There was something sexy about being a hood although it sur-
prises me because a split skull is not intelligent.

Sal Mineo and James Dean.
I wanted to be the scream that their victims
Made in the fabricated shade.

I wanted to die like Susan Hayward was executed
In "I Want to Live.

Sure, we all want to live like our victims wanted to live
But none of us are given the choice.

Words

So I am a block of words. I am refrigerated ideas in ice cube
trays of language run wild into its own cold stasis.

Life is sentences and I am sentenced
To the space between
A poet's commas.

It's not that I don't understand my words but that my words have
a life of their own in the suburbs of family life.

If words are ice than ice is meaning
And the cold result
Of the mind
Is scribbled on pineapple rind.

I am the frosty in snowman and the articulation in erudite lan-
guage so that I am the intelligence of what is missing.

I am a snowball. I am the other side of winter.

It Is So Easy

You specialize in hating Nazis. It is so easy. They are so obvious. You pat yourself on the back for being anti-fascist. Like that's a big deal. Like hating mass murderers is a salutation to goodness. So you go from hating the right to praising the left. You don't see that communists are also Nazis. They have killed more people in Russia, China, Vietnam, Cambodia and recently Venezuela than Hitler and the gang. When my parents visited Moscow in the seventies they were followed around by KGB agents and had to brush their teeth with coca cola. There were lines at all the food stores. Communism is an evil game that takes credit for its good intentions. It is failed optimism. It is theft from the successful to give goodies to the unaccomplished. It is spreading my wealth into your pockets. It is hating McCarthy for giving a few screenwriters a hard time for their anti-capitalist sentiments. It is a defense of Stalin's multi-million murders. It is traitors stealing American pie from the real chefs.

Lying Like Sadness

I have listened to nothing and said a lot about it into the invisible phone of non-communication.

You come to be like the truth
But you are always lying
Like sadness.

Everywhere the round turns round until I am flattened out by the feeling of vertigo in the sun beneath the shades.

What difference does your difference make
When I am falling in love with my shoes
As I step on my head.

The only thing good about meeting you is meeting you and the surprise that you could be so wonderful when you are not even trying.

A Life of Minor Crime

I have done what I have done which is some more
Than a lot and grander than not.
I am here like beer.
I hate beer.
I drank thirteen bottles of Mexican beer
At sixteen years old
At the World's fair in Flushing.
I vomited for an hour in a bathroom stall
I never drank beer again.
I don't like to get high.
I am high naturally.
I am the beauty of a magnificent intellect
Like the faces on Mt. Rushmore.
At fourteen I was detained for stealing trinkets
From the gift shop in North Dakota.
That's where I started my life of crime which
Ended in tax evasion in 1991.
Two years with the Feds.
Some small stuff.
I could have been larger than small,
A killer,
A thriller.
Your worst dream and the throat's caught scream.

Pope Francis

Time passes but is not here in that it is just a measurement
Of something on the outside looking in.
I am a window into myself.
I am the living room.
I am the fireplace.
I am the substance of my disappearance.
I fork out pieces of myself and feed them to the universe.
So my life is almost over.
So my stomach is full with my days
And I have eaten myself.
I growl.
I have gas.
I am a whole meal spread out on my wife's Flora Danica dishes.
The Pope ate off a similar spread.
Pope Francis is very proper except when he comes to covering
up
Pedophilia.
He pretends that he is a very moral man.
He was praised for the irrelevance of living in small quarters.
He wants no borders.
Maybe that's so he can sneak more children into his lair.

Conscience

I don't have a social conscience because conscience implies
failure
To take action against a sea of clichés.
Protest is a failure to take heart
And to shout at soul mates as if they were different.
In the fifties I marched against racism.
Now when racism is dead the blacks finally protest against
Cops arresting black felons.
Their timing is off.
I'm white and did two years in the Federal Joint.
Who cares?
It's usually whites who know nothing about jail who protest.
On my last day of jail I cried because I was unsure about what
I'd do when I got home.
Jail had become my family.
Protest is protest against things as they are
And if you can't accept acceptance you become a dwarf-planet
Like Pluto.

9/11

The days pass me by like shreds of newspaper in the wind.
I am not an Indian.
I am not Elizabeth Warren.
I am a non-violent sheik who places his cheek
Against the towel on his head.
I am hidden.
I am power.
I steal lives from my people by the hour.
I am all that matters.
I gather myself up into my narcissism and ride my camel
Like a sailboat.
I carry oil in a bowl on my head
And am as rich as a bitch is nastiness in a relationship.
I do not have Islamophobia.
I am not afraid of them.
I am waiting for western civilization to get out of bed
And pop our vengeance for 9/11
And the victims who jumped to their deaths from good jobs.

My Sock

The loneliness of night is the denouement of day.
Doody, did I say.
Quit joking.
i am enthralled by finding myself
Alone
Dejected
In a diving suit without a helmet.
I have failed making a big go in the small city and
Find that I am a faucet dripping down the drain.
I come and go like disappearance.
I am the forward motion of a broken ankle
Tripping into depression.
I take off my sock to share the view of my injuries
To those who hate me.

On the Edge

Sometimes I want to kill myself in a vague act of suicidal rage.
Other times I want to put myself
On a pedestal and become the statue
That was frozen in its own rage.
I am not this.
I am that.
I am whatever the mood shines on my disaffection.
It doesn't matter what I am
When I am almost always not,
A dash from the high school track to my girlfriend's bedroom.
I have led so many lives
That I can't recognize myself in my variable crowd.
I am carrying a picket sign in a protest march
Against protests.
There's not much sense in all this nonsense.
I find solace in confusion and solidarity in insanity.

Carousel

The hoofs are patting on the ground as they run away from the evidence of their future death. I am a horse. I am its neighing. I am the glue that will gather loveliness into its own mica. I am the shiny stones cracked on the sidewalk that are not shit but schist. I have a lot of problems. I don't know what they are. I am the carousel without the horses that twirls emptiness around. I am the brass ring that a boy sticks in his pocket. I am known for being unknowable and I am the dream you failed to have when you took narcotics. I want to get along with you but you keep getting along down the block into your own ego. Time is what time was and the present is a bite out of the past.

Night Driver

I didn't have a driver's license but when I was seventeen
I wanted to kill myself in my dad's Lincoln.

President Kennedy was shot in a dark blue Lincoln.
I didn't care about him.
I was a selfish kid.
I didn't cry when they announced over the loud speaker
At school
That he was dead.

Kennedy had nothing to do with me and I was me,
Not him,
Not bullets in the head.

I had sneaked out at three in the morning
And was cruising Great Neck.
I wanted to slip down onto the floor
And hold the gas pedal with my hand while

I crashed into a parked car,
A tree.

I wanted to bang myself up into the next dimension
And die like a dent in consciousness.

I was hurt by youth.

I wanted to break myself more because I couldn't imagine
Salving the pain with idle chatter and rah-rah speeches.

I Am Christ

I walk across the water on holey pontoons. I am Christ. I am peanut butter and jelly, a good moral snack, a funky return to my youth. You know me. I know you. I am God in a raincoat catching the drizzle down of sins. You visit the holes in my palms and feel the pain of my pacification. I sermonized on the mount and it got me nowhere. I convinced you that I wanted to be hurt and suffocated on aphorisms. So you hurt me for the fun of it and I feel the blood in my eyes. I don't like the showiness of it all. I want to suffer in silence among the basket weavers who carry my pain. I don't want to retreat from mankind's cruelty and be a flower in a garden of delights and lights and I might be the God that I am.

Pick You Up

I was only joking because I don't feel anything seriously
Down in my gut.
I don't want to be a self-recriminating slut.
When I was young I used to drink Robitussin to get high.
High was low.
I liked being the space beneath my sock
And the sweat
Of wool.
I no longer know the meaning of meaning
And wander around like a face that's been slapped.
I am numb.
I am the sound of a failed engine.
I will sit in your driveway and pick you up.
You are my date for life.
We will kiss under the bridge to show that we are connected
By the abutments and the road burying us beneath it.

Blinders of Blindness

Ignoring terrorism is its own form of terrorism. Wearing blinders
leads to blindness.
I hate the blind.
They can't see me.
I don't exist without their laying their eyes on my face,
My moods,
My being who I am.
If you see the Palestinian as a freedom fighter
Rather than someone blowing up a hundred people
In a marketplace
Than you need a cane just to walk to the bathroom
To enema your horrible sympathies.
You always side with the killers.
You are a victim of your stupidity and a murderer of innocence.
I should have spoken up against you before you lit the fuse.
I have become an honorary killer Palestinian.
I am that corner of your guilt that hides in the far reaches of my
stupidity.

Clue

Love is the absence of purpose in the wandering vagueness of
impulse.
It goes nowhere as it is drawn
To a strange conclusion.
What does it mean?
What do you mean in my insertion into your personality
And my attempt to grasp your meaning?
I know you.
I don't really have a clue.
But I shake the Clue Board and find
Miss Scarlet and Mrs. White.
You are the fabulous roll of the dice.
If I could play with you forever I would welcome never dying.

Death

I didn't believe in God until I spoke to him and he spoke back.
He said, "I don't exist."

That was nice to know because I didn't want to think
That there was a God who did such a botched up job.

God invented death to avoid over-population.
He could have just rescinded the penis and the vagina.

He could have made the organs work on a partial basis.
He could have reduced the population
And stopped death.

He didn't have to kill all of us so that we didn't have to experi-
ence
The sadness of buying new coffins.

God didn't have to be proud like death in our elimination.
We are bowels.
We come out from our intellects on to the other side of "De-
pends."

God has fed us his special brand of laxatives.
The situation stinks.

Broken Riding

The loneliness of night is the denouement of day.

I am enthralled by finding myself
Alone,
Dejected
In a diving suit without a helmet.

I have failed making a big go in the small city and
Find that I am a faucet drip down the drain.

I come and go like disappearance.
I am the forward motion of a broken ankle
Riding into depression.

I go to the hospital to teach them about injuries.

Me and Yourself

What you don't like about me is yourself which you project onto
my personality
In a jealous eyelash that wets your eye.

You can't see me for whom I am.
You see me for yourself.
I am you.

You couldn't get so angry at a stranger.
It's not that you hate me but
That you can't separate yourself from my relationship to you.

We are emotional twins.
It's as if we were born together looking like each other's'
personalities.

Crucified

You confessed to crimes you didn't commit
To try to avoid those that you did.

You are guilty of what you are hiding and taking
Negative credit for other sins
Is a Halloween mask.

If you would stand up for your standing
As a degenerate
The trees next to you would not be chopped down.

The world would be right.
Everything would be rising like a career
And the future would be magnificent and flexible.
I admit what I did.

Which is nothing
Which is the sins of mankind that dig like nails
into my palms.

Confusion

I have seen the coming of darkness and was thrilled
That light could be black
That failure could beam
That I seemed more than I was to the average jerk.

I'm special
Like three eggs and bacon at a discount.

You know me for whom I am not
And I know you for the chink you enter in my brain.

You occupy the space of antagonism
In the wisdom
Of intellectual infiltration.

I am bored with myself and find you like a fish
On a boat's deck.

In my teens I had a sailboat on the Long Island Sound.
I don't like waves.
So many humans send me into the wake of inevitable confusion.

Necklace

I pretend these rocks are gems and that I am rich
From the absence of value.

You come and go.
So?

I don't know whether direction is satisfaction
Or mis-stepping on the lily pods.

What if I drown?

What will be the sound of gurgling and choking?

Tomorrow will have infinite value
Like a diamond-emerald necklace on my rich date.

Toy Store

I am lost in an attic of miniatures. Time goes into the trash bin of confusion and I can't tell whether I am coming or going or am gone. I get lost at a toy store where I am trying to pick what is or isn't mine. I print on the back of my shirt— "Toys are Us." But I am not fun or frolic or a plastic jeep. I am a child's dream. I mean and I don't mean. I am a jolly good scream in a cave where the unconscious drips like stalactites from the walls. I was at Howe's Caverns fifty years ago. That's where I first experienced claustrophobia. I am a distraction. I am an abstraction. I don't really know who I am as I approach the circle of Alzheimer's with a square printed on my chest. Is this my preparation for death? Will it be easier on me to get out of here if I am already out of it? I look backwards and see forwards. I lift my eyes above my shoulder.